The Amazing Adve of MouMou & Fri

GW00865900

Series 1- Episode 2

Created and Written by

Sara Momtaz

MAPLE
PUBLISHERS

The Amazing Adventures of MouMou & Friends: Series 1 - Episode 2

Author: Sara Momtaz

Copyright © Sara Momtaz (2022)

The right of Sara Momtaz to be identified as author of this work has been asserted by the author in accordance with section 77 and 78 of the Copyright, Designs and Patents Act 1988.

First Published in 2022

ISBN: 978-1-915492-42-5 (Paperback)
       978-1-915492-43-2 (E-Book)

Book cover design, Illustrations and Book layout by:
    White Magic Studios
    www.whitemagicstudios.co.uk

Published by:
    Maple Publishers
    1 Brunel Way,
    Slough,
    SL1 1FQ, UK
    www.maplepublishers.com

A CIP catalogue record for this title is available from the British Library.

All rights reserved. No part of this book may be reproduced or translated by any form or by any means, electronic or mechanical, including photocopying, recording or by any information storage and retrieval system without written permission from the author.

EPISODE 2
MORE THAN A RACE

DEDICATION

For my dearest Amani. Love is too small a word
to describe my feelings for you. You are my
inspiration, my joy, my light and my true happiness.
I won't change you for the world but
I will change the world for you.

My endless love, Mummy

"Come on Harvey, keep up! I don't want to be late," said MouMou. After all the chaos of the book hunt, MouMou was keen to get to school and return Ava's book to her. "I'm sorry MouMou, I just can't move much with this ridiculous outfit that mummy has made me wear!" replied Harvey.

Well, it's probably a good time to let you know that MouMou's mummy is absolutely obsessed with dressing Harvey in the most extravagant and flamboyant outfits!

"Hahaha." laughed MouMou hysterically. "Yes, Mr Officer, today's ensemble is particularly ridiculous!"

Having finally arrived at school, MouMou spotted Ava and ran up to her to return her book.

"Thanks, Ava," said MouMou, "the book really was as good as you said it would be! By the way, are you ready for later? I'm so excited, Ava, I can't wait!" Ava replied, "I don't think I will be able to join MouMou, no one seems to ever want me on their team because of my wheelchair." The girls were talking about the school's Sports Day which was happening that afternoon.

"Ricky has been making fun of me all day, saying no one will want me to join in because I would slow them down."

Ava uses a wheelchair because it helps her to get around. She has Cerebral Palsy and is an absolute whizz in her wheelchair, which is part of her everyday life.

"Where's Ricky?" yelled MouMou angrily. "How dare he make fun of you like that? Wait 'til I see him!" "Oh, forget him, MouMou." advised Harvey "Come on let's get our things ready, they will start Sports Day soon," and off they went to prepare.

Everyone was out on the field, and the team captains were about to call the names of the kids they wanted on their teams. Ricky was one of the captains and, sure enough, Ava was the last to be picked and ended up on Ricky's team by chance. Ricky had told his team not to let Ava join in and just let her watch while the rest of them competed with the other teams in the competition.

Ava was very upset and unfortunately MouMou couldn't console her as she was on one of the other teams.

The last event of the day was the 50-metre sprint and Ricky, who was very good at sports, was running the race for his team. MouMou was also running in the race for her team. She wasn't the fastest, but her captain Adam wanted everyone to take part and so assigned MouMou to the sprint because he knew she loved to run. Harvey, who was jumping around with extreme enthusiasm, was cheering, "Come on, MouMou! You got this, let's go!" Ava, too, was rooting for MouMou even though they were on different teams.

"Ok, kids" announced the PE Teacher, "take your marks, get set...........go!!!!!!!!!!!!" And off they went. As expected, Ricky had a tremendous start and went flying down the track. All the kids were cheering their team-mates on, and Harvey and Ava joined to root for MouMou. Ricky was way ahead of everyone and looked back with a huge arrogant smirk on his face.

MouMou noticed that Ricky's shoelaces were undone. She warned, "Ricky, be careful! Your shoes!" And before he knew it, Ricky tripped and fell with a huge thump to the ground and rolled around until he eventually came to a halt!

By now, all the others had crossed the finish line, and MouMou came in second. The PE Teacher ran over to Ricky who was crying in agony with pain and was eventually taken to hospital in an ambulance. It turned out he had fractured both legs and his hip. He had his leg in a cast, and needed crutches and a wheelchair to help him get around.

The next day at school, everyone was talking about what happened. "Poor Ricky," said Ava, "he must be in a lot of pain and he won't be able to play all the sports he loves for a few months until he fully recovers." "Yes," agreed MouMou, "if only he had tied his shoelaces properly in the first place!"

Later that evening at home, Enzo was helping MouMou with her Maths homework and said, "You know, MouMou, maybe now Ricky will no longer make fun of Ava." "What do you mean, Enzo?" asked MouMou. "Well," explained Enzo, "now that he will spend the next couple of months in a wheelchair, he will have a better understanding of Ava's everyday life and will appreciate that regardless of what we can and can't do, we must be kind to each other." "Yes, you're absolutely right Enzo," agreed MouMou, "after all, we all belong."

The phone rang and it was Ava. "You won't believe what just happened, MouMou," said Ava. "Ricky and his mum just came to our house and he apologised for making fun of me. He said that whether someone is in a wheelchair temporarily or permanently, we shouldn't be mean to them or treat them differently. It doesn't matter whether we can run, walk or push ourselves along, what matters is that we move along together."

"That's amazing!" exclaimed MouMou. "I'm so happy to hear that Ricky has finally understood that we are more alike than we are different! Both girls then shouted out, "WE ALL BELONG"!

Stay tuned for more of the amazing
adventures of MouMou and friends!

THE END

Oh yeah! We just remembered that we didn't tell you about MouMou's superpowers! We were so excited about the wonders of Sports Day that it simply slipped our mind! Never mind, everything will be revealed in the next episode, promise!

You guys must have already guessed one of them – MouMou can talk to animals. She has two more, which you can discover in the next story. See you then for some more fun and games!

Lightning Source UK Ltd.
Milton Keynes UK
UKHW051842031222
413276UK00008B/55

9 781915 492425